choose
kindness

30 DEVOTIONS FOR CULTIVATING A KIND HEART

Published by LifeWay Press®

ISBN 978-1-0877-4256-4
Item 005831565
Dewey Decimal Classification Number: 242
Subject Heading: DEVOTIONAL LITERATURE / BIBLE STUDY AND TEACHING / GOD

publishing team

Director, Student Ministry
Ben Trueblood

Manager, Student Ministry Publishing
John Paul Basham

Editorial Team Leader
Karen Daniel

Content Editor
Stephanie Cross

Production Editor
Brooke Hill

Graphic Designer
Kaitlin Redmond

Printed in the United States of America

Student Ministry Publishing
LifeWay Resources
One LifeWay Plaza
Nashville, Tennessee 37234

We believe that the Bible has God for its author; salvation for its end; and truth, without any mixture of error, for its matter and that all Scripture is totally true and trustworthy. To review LifeWay's doctrinal guideline, please visit www.lifeway.com/doctrinalguideline.

table of contents

intro

As we live our day-to-day lives, it's so easy to get caught up in the details; the chores, the school projects, the Friday night football games, the Saturday shopping trips, the college visits and applications, the volleyball practices, the church choir productions—and the list goes on. While none of these things are bad in and of themselves, they can distract us from what God has called us to do: to focus on God and others rather than self.

This idea of focusing on others is completely counter cultural. It was in Jesus' day, too. Our world is obsessed with individualism, meism, or a self-focused worldview. For some people, even acts of kindness are self-serving. There are people who love to show off to the world their virtue or good works and acts of kindness—particularly on social media. This is called virtue signaling. Basically, people point out their own "right" view while shaming those who believe differently or don't act on their beliefs.

In such an individualistic world, it's easy to get caught up in what's best for us. We all want to be set apart, known as the unique individuals that we are. While the Bible teaches us that we are each created with uniqueness and were made to be set apart for Him, this is not an individualistic view. We are not set apart to serve ourselves or for our own benefit, but to serve the Lord and others with a glad heart. The Christian life is centered in the importance of community with God and others. And community means we show kindness to everyone around us—especially when they can't give anything in return.

Over the next 30 days, we'll learn that kindness isn't just about the cool, nice things we do that we post on social media from time to time. True kindness is an overflow of God's Spirit dwelling within His people and working through our lives. This is real and life changing kindness that is expected and commanded of those who love Jesus.

These 30 devotions will challenge you. They will cause you to examine your heart and your view of the poor and marginalized. They will reveal God's heart for the people society so often despises. And they will help you cultivate a true, Spirit-led and heart-felt kindness based in loving God and others rather than in looking good.

getting started

This devotional contains 30 days of content, divided into sections that answer a specific question about kindness. Each day is broken down into three elements—discover, delight, and display—to help you answer core questions related to Scripture.

discover | This section helps you examine the passage in light of who God is and determine what it says about your identity in view of that. Included here is the key passage, focus Scripture, along with illustrations and commentary to guide you as you study.

delight | In this section, you'll be challenged by questions and activities that help you see how God is alive and active in every detail of His Word and your life. You'll be guided to ask yourself about what the passage means for your relationship with God.

display | Here's where you really take action. Display calls you to apply what you've learned through each day's study.

prayer | Each day also includes a prayer activity in one of the three main sections.

Throughout the devotional, you'll also find extra articles and activities to help you connect with the topic personally, such as Scripture memory verses, additional resources, and questions.

day 1

A SPIRIT OF KINDNESS

discover|

> As we begin studying kindness, let's start with confession before God. Do you desire to be kind? Ask the Holy Spirit to prepare your heart for these devotions. Commit to God your willingness to grow in kindness.

READ COLOSSIANS 3:12-13.

Therefore, as God's chosen ones, holy and dearly loved, put on compassion, kindness, humility, gentleness, and patience. — Colossians 3:12

Maybe you've seen a girl be kind to a her friend, then turn around and gossip about her when she walks away. You'd probably consider that person's kindness fake, right? Well, kindness flows from the Holy Spirit's presence in the Christian's heart, so godly kindness cannot be faked.

It's also important to know that kindness isn't what saves us. People who've trusted in Jesus as their Savior practice kindness because they are saved, but they are not saved by acts of kindness. Christians intentionally "put on" kindness, because the Holy Spirit is in us. While someone whose heart is far from God could be used by God to show kindness, these acts of kindness do not save him or her.

Look closely at the first five words of these verses. It all begins with belonging to God. Compassion, kindness, humility, and the other attributes flow from the fact that we belong to God. Notice how logically consistent this is, given the fact that we are, according to verse 12, "holy and dearly loved." We are loving and kind toward others because God is loving and kind toward us.

delight |

Are you certain that you belong to God? If not, confess today that Jesus is Lord (Rom. 10:9) and then tell your ministry leader!

What is the connection between the kindness God showed you in your sin and the kindness God calls you to show others?

Before you had the God called Kindness you were just being kind to be nice. But now it's what God calls you do.

How is an act of kindness that flows from the Holy Spirit in our hearts better than an act of kindness done for the sake of looking good in front of others?

Because when we try to look good we arn't actually wanting to be kind we just wan't attention. But when we do it for God he calls us to do good.

display |

When we grasp the cosmic fact that God loves us dearly, it changes everything. Seeing ourselves as God's beloved helps us see others through God's eyes and elevates the view we have of other people. We begin to see others the way God sees them. God loves the world (John 3:16), and those who belong to Him should love the world, too. So, acts of kindness flow naturally out of God's love in us.

Plan an anonymous act of kindness; a favor, gift, or encouraging word you will give to someone this week. Do it without seeking to receive any credit.

Ask the Holy Spirit to guide you as you examine your heart: When might you be tempted to treat someone with kindness to make yourself look good rather than to make God look good?

LOVING KINDNESS

discover|

READ 1 CORINTHIANS 13:4-7.

Love is patient, love is kind. Love does not envy, is not boastful, is not arrogant.
— 1 Corinthians 13:4

If you are a Christian, then the Holy Spirit lives within you. If the Holy Spirit lives within you, then you have been uniquely gifted and called by the Holy Spirit for something important. You also have a unique set of spiritual gifts for ministry. It's important to use these gifts to show love rather than for personal gain.

While we often hear this verse read at weddings, in its original context, it is about how we use spiritual gifts. These gifts are to be used in a humble, patient, and kind way to help others and glorify God. We choose kindness because the Spirit of God is in us, and we expect to receive absolutely nothing in return.

Talk to God, praying for His will to be done. Ask Him to reveal to you the good works He has prepared for you this week. Then, ask Him for the strength to follow through with these opportunities to show kindness, knowing that your intention is not to receive recognition or return favors.

delight |

What is love without patience like? What about love that is marked by envy?

When people post about their acts of kindness on social media, what's your initial reaction? What might this indicate about their attitude toward kindness?

Describe an act of kindness done for personal gain or recognition rather than love. When have you been tempted to show this type of kindness?

display |

Living out kindness as a fruit of the Spirit requires patience. Prepare your heart: Your acts of kindness could met with indifference or even hostility. Living out kindness also requires sincere love in your heart for the people you serve.

Check your heart for any envy. Read your own past social media posts for anything that might sound self-centered or braggy. Keep an eye out for any feelings of arrogance that might come after you've acted in kindness.

Think about a girl who tests your patience or who may just need a friend. List some ways you can show kindness to her today.

If you've bragged about the ways you've shown kindness in the past—seek God's forgiveness and apologize to anyone who may have been affected. Then, take a look at what Jesus said in Matthew 6:1-3.

day 3

THE POISON APPLE

discover |

READ PROVERBS 26:23-28.

When he speaks graciously, don't believe him, for there are seven detestable things in his heart. — *Proverbs 26:25*

King Solomon wrote much of the Book of Proverbs. Though he was far from perfect, the wisdom he shared came straight from God. As Solomon trained his sons to become kings, he taught extensively on wisdom—which begins with a fear (reverence, respect, and awe) of the Lord (Prov. 1:7). In Proverbs 26, he warned his sons about the hateful person who "disguises himself with his speech and harbors deceit within" (Prov. 26:24).

Solomon would go on to say this hateful person—with a "flattering mouth" (Prov. 26:28)—would ultimately dig a pit and fall into it (v. 27). That's quite the picture, right? Solomon also said this person's evil would eventually be revealed (v. 26). Tragically, this happens far too often—and sometimes it even happens in the church!

Take a second and think about the fact that the flattering speech of this hateful person is given with "smooth lips" (v. 23). In other words, this person would appear to be incredibly kind. This is fake kindness, which isn't kindness at all. Kindness must be genuine, or it's just like the apple Snow White took from the evil queen: It may look appealing, but it's dangerous.

delight |

Where are you most tempted to fake kindness when you really wish you could tell the truth?

Who have you misled in the past by giving flattering compliments that you didn't actually mean?

What effect might this false kindness have on your credibility in the future?

display |

No matter how people treat you be prepared to choose kindness. Protect your heart from being deceived by empty words of flattery from people who appear kind but are really just manipulating you. Watch for this same behavior in your own heart. Remember that your actions and words of kindness are strongest when they are not rooted in the Holy Spirit's prompting and not what you stand to gain from the person to whom you are showing kindness.

Are you showing favoritism to people who could make you more popular, or are you showing kindness to absolutely everyone, regardless of what they could do for you? Evaluate your motives each time you show kindness to someone today. Journal what happens in your heart when you show genuine kindness to someone who has nothing to offer you.

Ask God to give you discernment into your own heart; to alert you when you are about to give kind words that are really just intended to avoid the awkwardness of the truth, cover your own tracks, or put yourself on good terms with someone who could do something for you.

EVERYONE CAN BE KIND

discover |

READ ACTS 28:1-6.

The local people showed us extraordinary kindness. They lit a fire and took us all in, since it was raining and cold. — Acts 28:2

This beautiful scene was made possible by God's ministry through Paul to the Roman centurion (a commanding soldier) onboard his ship that had just wrecked onto the island of Malta. The other soldiers had planned to kill the prisoners, but this centurion liked Paul and decided that the prisoners should swim or drift ashore. Paul's gospel testimony saved lives! However, they still had to survive on Malta. But Paul had absolute confidence that everyone would survive because of a vision God gave him (27:14,23-26).

The local people of Malta lit a fire for them and took them in because it was raining and cold. This kindness was unprompted, and the shipwreck survivors would not likely be able to repay it, having tossed valuables overboard (28:18-19).

What a beautiful legacy! The people of Malta displayed incredible kindness to people who couldn't repay them and their hospitality is recorded in the Bible for all-time. Here's the thing: Everyone can be kind, Christian or not.

> Prayerfully reflect on your time of greatest need, considering who showed you kindness and how. Then, make a commitment to God that you will be ready to show this same kindness to those in need around you!

delight |

In what ways are Paul's vision from God before the shipwreck (Acts 27:23-26) and the kindness shown by the people of Malta connected?

The people of Malta were not Christians (Acts 28:3-5) or not yet Christians (28:7-10). What does this say about the idea that God only works through Christians to show kindness to those who need it?

The word "extraordinary" in this verse is super important. What is the difference between ordinary kindness and extraordinary kindness?

display |

These incredibly kind people went through great trouble to help shipwrecked strangers, and the Lord blessed them abundantly as a result of the ministry of one lowly prisoner in their midst. God would heal their leader's father through Paul's hands (28:7-10) and then heal everyone else on the island who was sick! But they couldn't have known this as they showed extraordinary kindness to the shipwrecked strangers. You have seen the legendary kindness of the people at Malta. Now, it's your turn.

Work with your parent(s) or guardian(s) to come up with ideas and gather items to meet someone's physical needs. Pray that God would give you the opportunity to share the gospel as you serve others. Don't settle for ordinary kindness; instead, show extraordinary kindness!

People are often fighting unseen battles every day. Think about the new girl, the quiet girl, the girl who keeps to herself. Consider ways you can reach out to her and show her extraordinary kindness today.

Choose Kindness

day 5

WHAT GOES AROUND

discover|

> Start your prayer with praise and thanksgiving; letting gratitude for all the ways God provides for you outshine what troubles you. Then, ask God to root out any cruelty in you and for kindness to reign in your heart.

READ PROVERBS 11:17.

A kind man benefits himself, but a cruel person brings ruin on himself.

The wisdom of Proverbs could have been written yesterday, but these timeless truths are thousands of years old. The Book of Proverbs is filled with sound advice, although following it doesn't guarantee success. These little poetic couplets are life-hacks from God. You could live ten lifetimes and learn only a fraction of these truths the hard way. Or you could read the Proverbs, apply them to your life, and make the most of the only life you have.

Today's Proverb is one of several that contrasts the kind person with the cruel. Look closely at the first half of verse 17. It is almost counter-intuitive. How does someone who does kind things for others benefit himself? This verse is not to be confused with the idea of "karma." It also should not reconfigure your motivation for kindness. Kindness that is shown for the sole reason of benefiting oneself is manipulation, but kindness shown as an overflow of the Holy Spirit's presence in your life honors God. It also does benefit us in the long-run. Likewise, a girl who is cruel to others will ultimately bring ruin that will crash down on her.

delight |

What's your natural response when someone does something kind for you or says something kind to you?

In what ways have acts of kindness in your past come back to bless you later?

How have you seen acts of cruelty repaid in the end?

display |

Because you live in a world where not everyone submits to the Word of God, you will encounter cruelty. When you do, remember Proverbs 11:17. In that moment, avoid the temptation to take delight in the ruin that comes upon the cruel. Rather, take comfort in the first half of the verse—assurance that you are on God's track.

Show kindness to someone today, not because you hope to reap this promised benefit, but just because you love Jesus and He told us to love our neighbors.

Take a look at Romans 12:18-19. Knowing that the cruel will experience ruin, show grace when others are cruel to you and express gratitude to God when your own kindness benefits you.

On an index card, write out the words *Kindness benefits me.* Keep this card with you. When you are tempted to not treat someone kindly, take out this care and read it as a reminder to always choose kindness.

Therefore, as God's chosen ones, holy and dearly loved, put on compassion, kindness, humility, gentleness, and patience, bearing with one another and forgiving one another if anyone has a grievance against another. Just as the Lord has forgiven you, so you are also to forgive.

COLOSSIANS 3:12-13

day 6

REFLECT HIS LIGHT

discover|

God already knows about your sin, but loves you anyway. So, confess freely to Him anything on your heart. Trust in the atoning work of Christ, who paid for your sin with His perfect life and rose again in victory over it.

READ EPHESIANS 2:1-10.

He also raised us up with him and seated us with him in the heavens in Christ Jesus, so that in the coming ages he might display the immeasurable riches of his grace through his kindness to us in Christ Jesus. —Ephesians 2:6-7

When people post their opinions about a particular issue—pointing out their own "right" view while shaming those who believe differently or don't act on their beliefs—it's called virtue signaling. It's a fake righteousness; show put on for others, not necessarily a belief personally lived. The first words in today's passage would likely be considered offensive by a culture plagued with virtue-signaling: Before Christ, we were actually dead in sin.

But this beautiful news reveals a critical difference between Christianity and every other worldview. While other religious worldviews try to tell us how to climb the mountain to heaven, Christianity sees us as dead and incapable of climbing at all! Instead, God reached down and raised us up from our sin.

As recipients of such endless grace, we are to reflect the light of God's loving kindness. We believe the gospel and are saved, but did none of the work. Salvation is an act of kindness from God that flows from the love He had for us even while we were dead in sin. He did this ultimately for His own glory. As the recipients of the immeasurable riches of His grace (v. 7), that kindness reflects off of us and invites others who are still in darkness into the light of His gospel.

delight |

List a few images or ideas that come to mind when you hear the word dead. Then, reflect in a journal about how it affects you to know that you were dead in your sins but made alive in Christ.

Highlight the words "raised us up with him and seated us with him" (v. 6). This is past tense. As one scholar put it, "God has decided to do it, and it is as good as done. We just have to wait for a few years until it happens."[1] How does this affect your faith and desire to share that faith with others?

display |

If you have been taking credit for your own salvation, attributing it to righteous acts you have performed in the past, ask God to help you remove that desire from your heart and give it over to Him. Thank Jesus for raising you up when you were dead in sin.

God already looks at Christians as a part of His family through Jesus. What does this say about God's kindness toward you? Consider other Christians you might dislike or disagree with. How can you begin treating them with kindness—like they're already seated with Christ—just like God does?

JUST MERCY

discover |

READ TITUS 3:1-7.

But when the kindness of God our Savior and his love for mankind appeared, he saved us—not by works of righteousness that we had done, but according to his mercy—through the washing of regeneration and renewal by the Holy Spirit.
—Titus 3:4-5

Today's passage is a letter from Paul—inspired by the Holy Spirit—to Titus. Titus was called to appoint elders in towns all over the island of Crete, and Paul was writing instruction and encouragement. Today, these words hit us squarely in our sense of self-righteousness and have been extremely helpful for people who come from other faiths to belief in the true gospel of Jesus Christ.

Verse 4 changes everything. Since time began, people have been trying to save themselves, but we never have nor will we be able to. To the Pharisees of Jesus' day, this kind of teaching was so humbling that it was offensive. To the virtue-signaling culture of our day and to the false religions that teach salvation through works, it is just as offensive. To those who have placed their faith in Jesus, it is freedom.

> Thank God for His loving kindness. Thank Him for saving you, not because of your own works of righteousness, but just because of His mercy. Thank Him for washing away your sin, for bringing you from death in sin, and for making you brand new through the Holy Spirit.

delight |

List some of the words Paul used to describe what we were like before coming to know Christ. How does this affect your response to the truth that God loved us and sent a Savior for us?

Describe what you think and feel and how you react to reading that "he saved us—not by works of righteousness that we had done" (v. 5).

display |

This chapter of Titus describes how we struggle and work, give in to lies and forget the truth, and become slaves to what we love and enjoy. It reads like a blog post describing modern culture, but it was written nearly 2,000 years ago! The Word of God is always true and relevant. These words of freedom from legalism—the belief that you can save yourself with righteous acts—are still setting people free today.

Create a lock-screen of Titus 3:4-5 and save it as the background on your phone. Every time you see it, read it. Ask God to prepare your heart to share His truth with those who believe righteous acts gain spiritual favor or status—like those who follow Islam, Buddhism, or Mormonism.

If you use social media, share the lock-screen you created with your friends and followers. Ask God to help you respond with kindness to anyone who comments on your post.

day 8

GOD'S INEXHAUSTIBLE KINDNESS

discover |

READ PHILIPPIANS 4:10-20.

And my God will supply all your needs according to his riches in glory in Christ Jesus. — Philippians 4:19

Has anyone tried to encourage you by sharing Philippians 4:13 when you were facing a physically challenging situation? The verse says, "I am able to do all things through him who strengthens me." Well, today's passage helps us understand the truth about this truly misquoted verse. In context, Paul was thanking the church at Philippi for sending him a financial gift that met all of his needs and shared that he was acquainted with both poverty and plenty.

The Philippian believers may have thought they were just giving in support of Paul's ministry, but they were really giving "a fragrant offering, an acceptable sacrifice, pleasing to God (Phil. 4:18)." Verse 19 was Paul's comforting and prophetic response, which is also true for Christians today: The kindness God supplies for the receiver of the gift will be supplied to the giver as well.

> **Reflect on your life so far. Even if your family has struggled financially in the past, reflect on how God has always provided. Rest in the comfort that comes from knowing God's kindness will supply all of your needs. Thank Him for His provision.**

delight |

How might these words be especially comforting to people who don't have much but still faithfully give to the Lord?

What role does faith play when giving to God?

display |

Make it a point to rest in the comfort that comes from knowing your provisions ultimately come from God's "riches in glory in Christ Jesus." Set a timer and spend five minutes thanking your Provider whose riches never run dry. Spend every minute in a spirit of gratitude, glorifying God whose loving kindness never runs out!

After the timer goes off, reset it for five more minutes. Name five physical needs God meets for you every day. Spend one minute praising Him out loud for providing those specific things for you.

These words were originally written to Christians who had kindly given to Paul's ministry. Think about your church leadership, small group leaders, or missionaries supported by your church. What can you do to give to them—even if you can't give money?

REDEMPTION'S COST

discover |

Thank Jesus for paying for (atoning for) the sins of all who believe in Him, through His blood. As you would before taking the Lord's Supper at church, tell Him that you remember His broken body and atoning blood. Thank Him for His sacrifice.

READ EPHESIANS 1:7-10.

In him we have redemption through his blood, the forgiveness of our trespasses, according to the riches of his grace that he richly poured out on us with all wisdom and understanding. — Ephesians 1:7-8

As believers born into the New Testament era, we never had to travel to Jerusalem at Passover and sacrifice a lamb. We never saw its blood spilled symbolically on our behalf. The closest thing we have to this is the cup we drink at the Lord's Supper in remembrance of Jesus' blood. He is the ultimate Lamb—the Lamb of God who takes away the sin of the world (John 1:29). Our redemption came at a great cost: the blood of the Perfect One.

This redemption was not poured out thoughtlessly, but "with all wisdom and understanding" (v. 8). Jesus knew exactly what He was doing when He stood silent before His accusers and followed through with the crucifixion. He knew each one of us then—and our redemption is in Him and Him alone. It is the forgiveness of every last one of our trespasses according to His kindness.

delight |

Why do we need redemption (v. 7)?

What are the "riches of his grace" (v. 7)? How do these differ from worldly wealth?

What's your response to the truth that your redemption came as a result of Jesus' blood sacrifice on your behalf?

display |

Those of us who have this redemption through Christ are called to live like it—even if the people around us live differently. We forgive others because we have been forgiven, no matter what they've said or done. We invite others into the kindness of God because His forgiveness and redemption have been richly poured out on us from the riches of His grace.

Jot down the names of two people who you struggle to forgive and into God's kindness. Ask God to soften your heart toward them and help you forgive them. Write out one way you'll show kindness to each person this month.

Our kindness comes from the kindness God poured out on us. There's no room for pride in a heart humbled by His kindness. View every person you see the rest of the day through this lens. Recognize their need for His kindness and share the good news. Watch that same grace and kindness that was richly poured out on you be poured out onto others and give God 100 percent of the glory!

Choose Kindness

day 10

HELPER OR HYPOCRITE?

 discover |

READ ROMANS 2:1-4.

Or do you despise the riches of his kindness, restraint, and patience, not recognizing that God's kindness is intended to lead you to repentance?
— Romans 2:4

Today's culture loves to call out hypocrites. People on social media can quickly become a self-righteous mob, joyfully exposing others' wrongdoing and piling condemnation onto the humiliated people. But they fail to recognize the ironically wrong nature of the hateful frenzy itself. Paul warned his Roman readers of this very danger in verse 1.

It's a good idea to search our hearts and identify our own hypocrisy. But we need to guard our hearts from joining in the hoard of angry onlookers when someone else's hypocrisy is exposed. Paul reminded the Romans, and us, that neither the sinner nor the angry mob will escape God's judgment (v. 3).

God is patient with us and wants all people to repent (2 Pet. 3:9). But we must be careful not to delight in seeing another person fall. Every finger we point at the sinner in the center of a judgmental mob belongs to an equally qualified sinner. All of us will give an account before the same God whose kindness is designed to bring us all to repentance. God has called us to be helpers, not hypocrites.

delight |

When has God's kindness in your life led you to repentance?

When has the kindness of other believers pointed you back to God or into deeper relationship with Him?

Why is God's judgment based in truth while the judgment of a hateful mob is not (v. 2)?

Ask God to forgive you for the times when you joined hateful mob. Pray for God to remind you of these verses the next time you're tempted to join in. Ask for God's grace that overcomes the self-righteous desire to join in judging when someone is busted for something you have also done.

display |

Living according to God's Word will set you apart. In a world that is hungry to humiliate wrongdoers, reach out to the accused, saying, "I know what it is like to fall." This is radically counter-cultural and very gospel-centered. Look around you and see where you might reach out to someone who is hurting today.

Reflect on this question in your journal: Is God obligated to show us kindness? Why or why not?

Journal a prayer thanking God for His restraint when He saw you sin (v. 4). Thank God for His patience with you when you fell again and again.

What Kindness Does

When we think about the word kindness in the Bible, typically, this verse comes to mind: "Pleasant words are a honeycomb: sweet to the taste and health to the body" (Prov. 16:24). But kindness is meant for more than our words; kindness is about the way we treat others too.

Kindness Starts Here

Here's the thing: You cannot control what other people do. We live in a fallen world, so sometimes people do incredibly unkind things. With the help of the Holy Spirit, though, we can respond to others with both kindness and self-control (Gal. 5:22-23). Our responses are not mechanical; rather, they are guided by the very Spirit of the God who loves us. He is both our help and our ultimate example of loving kindness (John 14:26; Eph. 2:7). The truth is that we can choose kindness no matter what someone else does or fails to do. When it becomes especially difficult to be kind, first remember that God is and has been kind to us— even when we don't deserve it.

Kindness Is Good for Us

Not only do acts of kindness help others feel valued and seen, but they can also help us by increasing our mood and even our lifespan. Being kind to others even lowers our levels of stress, anxiety, pain, and depression. (https://www.dartmouth.edu/wellness/emotional/rakhealthfacts.pdf) This idea is found in Scripture, too. The Book of Proverbs says, "a kind man benefits himself" (11:17a), and some of those benefits include "life, righteousness, and honor" (21:21).

Kindness Is Good for Others

When we're kind to others, they experience more than a generous action or nice words. Take a look at these ten things the Bible says about what kindness does for others.

- Kindness shows love (1 Cor. 13:4).
- Being kind means extending forgiveness (Eph. 4:32).
- Kindness points others to Jesus (2 Cor. 6:3-13)
- Kindness expects nothing in return (Luke 6:35).
- God's kindness leads to repentance (Rom. 2:4).
- Kindness builds up others (Rom. 15:2).
- Being kind means welcoming and caring for even those we don't know (Acts 28:2).
- When we're kind, we care for the oppressed and marginalized (Isa. 1:17)
- Kindness rejoices with others (Rom. 12:15).
- Kindness restores (2 Sam. 9:7; Rom. 5:8).

Reflect

When have you done something kind for someone else and felt joy because of it?

How might being kind to others take our minds off of our own stress, depression, pain, or anxiety?

What are some ways kindness toward others reflects God's image into the world?

Which of the 10 effects of kindness stood out to you? Why?

If someone looked at your life over the last 24 hours, would they describe you as kind? Why or why not?

If not, how can you begin to choose kindness today?

day 11

BEGIN WITH FORGIVENESS

discover|

READ EPHESIANS 4:20-32.

And be kind and compassionate to one another, forgiving one another, just as God also forgave you in Christ. — Ephesians 4:32

Forgiveness sets us free. We are free to let go of past pain. We are free to move on from relationships and take the risk of trusting people again. Only the gospel makes this truly possible because only the gospel transforms people. It begins with accepting the reality that we are just as stained by sin as those who have sinned against us.

Refusing to forgive is from the old way; not the new way of life Jesus calls us to. But Paul instructed the Ephesians (and us) to take off the old way of living (v. 22). Grace is the only way a culture of imperfect people can move forward and grow—and there is no greater grace than that of God toward sinners.

If we want to practice kindness, then we need to be forgiving people. We are called to give what we have received. We have been freely forgiven, we also freely forgive.

delight |

In Matthew 5:7, Jesus said, "Blessed are the merciful, for they will be shown mercy." How is this verse similar to Ephesians 4:32?

Is it possible to be kind, but not compassionate? Why or why not?

display |

The truth is, we will be wronged and we have wronged others. We have a simple choice between forgiveness or giving in to bitterness. Remember God is the author of this beautiful concept. Remember the forgiveness He offers you begins with the sacrifice of the only One who has never wronged anyone. Commit to continuing God's work, choosing forgiveness over bitterness no matter what.

Think of a girl you have wronged. Reach out to her, apologize, and try to make things right unless doing so would wound her. No matter how she responds to you, choose kindness.

Allow the Holy Spirit to bring your heart to a place of true forgiveness toward those who have hurt you. Unless those who have wronged you have expressed a desire to hear your forgiveness articulated, there is no need to contact them and let them know you forgive them. In fact, this could do more harm than good. Sometimes others don't even realize they have hurt you in the first place.

> As you pray, imagine yourself setting down at God's feet the bitterness you may be holding against someone. Give to Him every wound on your heart from someone who hurt you. Then, abide in and trust the forgiveness Christ accomplished for you.

Choose Kindness

DO GOOD, ALWAYS

discover

> Ask God for a refreshing from His Spirit. Confess any sin
> you have been avoiding or pretending was nonexistent.
> Dwell in the peace that comes from knowing Christ's
> resurrection guarantees victory and atonement for every
> sin. Speak honestly with God about ways that you are
> weary, then prepare to be refreshed and encouraged.

READ GALATIANS 6:1-10.

Let us not get tired of doing good, for we will reap at the proper time if we
don't give up. Therefore, as we have opportunity, let us work for the good of all,
especially for those who belong to the household of faith. — Galatians 6:9-10

What if you pulled an all-nighter to finish a paper, but just stopped
before the conclusion? What if you dropped out of school one
week before graduation? What if you sang the entire solo except
the last line?

It is especially easy to grow tired of doing good and give up right
before the goal if you feel isolated and are not plugged into your
church. Your Christian walk is not just about you. It is the part you
play in the bigger picture of God's kingdom. Your unique spiritual
gifts and contributions are part of a team effort and that team is the
church. So, never give up, never walk alone, and work for the good
of your friends at church. You will find that your growing weariness
subsides when you lift up a fellow member of your family of faith.

delight |

List some examples of good works that may not show immediate results but could have a lasting impact for God's mission.

How can you practice working for the good of those in your local church? What about your youth group or small group?

There are huge theological implications to the words "as we have opportunity (v. 10)." Who provides these opportunities?

Why is it important to realize we are not the source of our good works?

display |

First Corinthians 15:58 says, "Therefore, my dear brothers and sisters, be steadfast, immovable, always excelling in the Lord's work, because you know that your labor in the Lord is not in vain." Your Spirit-filled acts of kindness are never meaningless. Know that you are not the only Christian in the world. God has surrounded you with others and they need encouragement too.

Make a list with the names of students and leaders in your church—including your pastor—who you can encourage today. God can use even a few quick to encourage them in a time of need.

UPSIDE DOWN

discover|

> Before you begin today's devotion, ask God to give you an open heart to what He has to say to you through His Word. Regardless of your relationship with your earthly father, You have a Heavenly Father who loves you and is ready to help you do something the world finds unbelievable.

READ LUKE 6:27-36.

Love your enemies, do what is good, and lend, expecting nothing in return. Then your reward will be great, and you will be children of the Most High. For he is gracious to the ungrateful and evil. — Luke 6:35

Christianity is distinct from other worldviews. In today's Scripture, Jesus said something radical—again. In case you haven't noticed already, God often calls us to do the opposite of what culture and our flesh tell us. He calls us to live in an upside down world.

Jesus acknowledged that, "Even sinners lend to sinners to be repaid in full" (v. 34). It is perfectly fair to expect to be repaid in full, but it's also perfectly Christ-like to give freely and expect nothing in return. He even calls His followers to love their enemies. This is counter-cultural and exactly what our world needs right now. It's easy to love those who love us. It's difficult to love those who are indifferent toward us or even despise us. While this might seem extreme to some, it's a basic part of our calling as Christians.

delight |

Have you ever let a friend borrow something that they didn't return? How did that make you feel?

While Jesus' teaching might be difficult and counter-cultural, He mentioned a "reward" (v. 35). What reward do you think Jesus is referring to here?

God is described as "the Most High" in verse 35. Because He is the Most High, He calls His people to a different standard. How does knowing that God is the Most High help you live out His standard?

display |

We are called to be daughters who act like our heavenly Father. Our Father freely gave, knowing we could never repay our debt. Our Father is gracious to us even when we are ungrateful. He even shows patient grace toward those who are evil, desiring that they come to repentance (2 Pet. 3:9). When we do what is good, love our enemies, show kindness as an overflow of the Spirit, and give without expecting a return, we are daughters who reflect our Father.

Keep your eyes open for opportunities to meet needs today. Then, step in, speak up, and serve well without expecting anything in return.

Journal about your faith in Jesus' promise of a great reward. Our faith is often tested. So, when the enemy discourages you, revisit this statement. It's not always easy to trust in Jesus' promise when we're tested.

day 14

BOLD HUMILITY

discover|

> Tell God how hallowed, or sacred, His name is to you. Praise Him for how great He is. As you grow in Him watch as both your troubles and your ego shrink in importance and prominence in your heart.

READ MICAH 6:8.

Mankind, he has told each of you what is good and what it is the LORD requires of you: to act justly, to love faithfulness, and to walk humbly with your God.

The prophet Micah did not mess around! He did not minimize the message God gave him or apologize for it. In today's verse, he called out all of humanity and his bold words still ring true today. As God's people, we know better. We know what is expected of us. These words should still be a focus in our hearts and lives today. God has called us to be boldly humble.

People are fickle—our emotions and moods change with the headlines or if we're hangry or sleepy. We are not the ultimate authority in life. Our opinions do not determine what is true or false. God is the only One who has the authority to determine what's right and wrong—and He has shared what is good and right through His Word. We know what is good and what the Lord requires of us because of His Word. In the New Testament, Jesus gave us only two commands: to love God and to love others (Matt. 22:37-40). This is kindness.

delight |

What are some practical ways you can act justly?

Since we are clearly called to walk humbly with our God, why do you think so many Christians struggle with humility?

display |

This Old Testament teaching is still true of God's character today. As New Testament believers, our obedience to the commands Jesus gave us—to love God and others (Matt. 22:37-40)—line up exactly with the calling of Micah 6:8 to act justly, love faithfulness, and walk humbly with our God.

It is good to grow and learn when presented with ideas we haven't encountered yet in God's Word. However, we have to be careful to make sure that every new idea we learn aligns with the truth of God's Word. It would be impossible to love faithfulness and walk humbly with God if we live guided by cultural morality. We must let God's word guide our interaction and posts on social media. Take a moment to review your recent posts. How do your recent posts reflect God's heart in today's verse?

When God gives you an opportunity to speak up about the gospel, let these words be branded on your heart. Speak kindly with the humility and boldness Micah called for.

day 15

PURE RELIGION

discover|

READ JAMES 1:19-27.

Pure and undefiled religion before God the Father is this: to look after orphans and widows in their distress and to keep oneself unstained from the world.
— James 1:27

One of the least-appreciated proofs of Jesus' divinity is the fact that His earthly half brother—one of the biological children of Joseph and Mary who used to rag on Jesus (John 7:2-9)—ultimately called Jesus "Lord." Think about what it might have been like to acknowledge that his brother was actually the Son of God—and was literally perfect. Jesus' brother was James, and he wrote the book we will learn from today.

The word "religion" brings up trauma for countless wounded souls. It evokes long legacies of meaningless rituals and rules that bring people no closer to God. However, today's Scripture brings this word back to its purest form. Out of the kindness the Holy Spirit produces in us, we look after orphans and widows in their distress.

Because we have been called out by God and set apart, we cannot possibly ever successfully blend in with the spiritual darkness around us. We are to be, "... blameless and pure, children of God who are faultless in a crooked and perverted generation, among whom you shine like stars in the world" (Phil. 2:15). We are to keep ourselves unstained from the world.

delight |

Think of how James defines "pure and undefiled religion." List some examples of this that you have seen.

How can we show kindness to the world and speak clearly and lovingly to those who don't know God while not being "stained" by the world?

display |

It is time to be real about your religion. The gospel purifies us and the Holy Spirit empowers us to live out our faith. Because you are a Spirit-filled Christian, kindness toward orphans and widows will result as fruit of your faith. This is what it means to live out the biblical definition, of the word *religion*.

Examine your life and the story it tells. Think about the way you spend your time and money. Sift through words you have said that came from worldly influences. Be honest in your heart before God and listen closely to the Holy Spirit's conviction. Seek to be an influence on the world rather than let the world be an influence you.

Work with your parent or guardian and a pastor or ministry leader to create a list of ways you can be a blessing to orphans in your community and widows in your church. Then, follow through, practicing godly kindness with pure and undefiled religion.

> Express to God your sincere intent not to compromise your personal holiness as you carry out His mission. Echo to God the words Jesus spoke to His disciples in Matthew 10:16 as you ask for God's help to be as shrewd as a serpent, but as innocent as a dove.

AND BE KIND AND
COMPASSIONATE
TO ONE ANOTHER,
FORGIVING ONE
ANOTHER,

JUST AS GOD
ALSO FORGAVE
YOU IN CHRIST.

EPHESIANS 4:32

day 16

OPPRESSION AND INSULTS

discover|

> Pray for those who do not currently have what they need for daily life. Ask God for opportunities to meet the needs of the most impoverished in your community.

READ PROVERBS 14:31.

The one who oppresses the poor person insults his Maker, but one who is kind to the needy honors him.

People caught up in a culture that does not practice godly kindness will show respect only to those who can give them something in return. So, a culture that lacks kindness will completely neglect the poor because the absolute poorest among us have nothing to give in return. As King Solomon imparted wisdom to his sons to prepare them to hopefully be Kings one day, he emphasized the obligation of a king to meet the needs of the poor by reminding them that even the poorest people belong to God.

Both the oppressor and the poor man have the same Maker—God. It's an insult to God Himself when we oppress other people whom He also lovingly created. Whether you have plenty, or little, the things of this world will do us no good when we stand before God. But when you are kind to the poor you imitate God—and this brings Him glory and honor.

delight |

God clearly cares for the poor. How can we honor God today, according to this passage?

How does it honor God when believers show kindness to those in greatest need?

display |

If your motivation in helping those who do not have as much as you is to look good or righteous, then you are looking to bring honor to yourself rather than God. However, when you do what Scripture says by honoring God through showing kindness to the poor, then this act of kindness is about so much more than your self-image.

While you may not be actively oppressing the poor, it's easy just to ignore them and assume it's not your problem. If you have opportunity to help someone but refuse, you've participated in ignoring their needs and this is an insult to God. Look around you: What needs to you see? Make a list of the needs you see and then write out every way you can think of that you might be able to care for those people. Then, highlight one practical way you will seek to show them kindness this month.

As God answers the prayer you prayed at the beginning of this devotion and you have opportunities to be kind to those in need, remember to see these people for who they are: people created by God—the same Maker who made you—in His image.

day 17

discover |

> Open with a prayer of gratitude for all that you have, even if it is not much compared to others.

MATTHEW 25:37-40.

"And the King will answer them, 'Truly I tell you, whatever you did
for one of the least of these brothers and sisters of mine, you did for me.'"
— *Matthew 25:40*

Christians have a greater obligation to care for the marginalized than the secular world possibly could. In fact, when non-Christians practice such kindness, they are actually borrowing from Christianity. All people are made in the image of God, but all people are also stained with sin. When one who does not know Christ does something from "the goodness of her heart," she is living out her original design—God's image—over her sin nature.

As a follower of Christ, the new life you have in Jesus calls you to live opposite of your sin nature at all times. Your reason for voluntarily feeding the hungry, giving a drink to the thirsty, pointing people to those who can help them when you can't, providing clothing to those who need it, and caring for the sick is because Jesus is your Lord. When you do these things, you bless Jesus. This is a higher calling than any self righteous behavior meant to impress others or make others think you're a good person.

delight |

Why is it important to show godly kindness "to the least of these" and not only to those who could pay you back or make you more popular?

Why do you think Jesus refer to the poor, sick, and imprisoned as His brothers and sisters?

How does Jesus' instruction to care for those in need apply to both those who have much and those who do not?

display |

There will always be girls who have more than you, so refuse to be taken in by the enemy's lie that you just need more stuff. The truth is that God will supply all of our needs, and sometimes, He uses us to fulfill one another's needs too! There are many ways to serve and ways we shouldn't serve. Take a look at the following list. Use one color to indicate things you should do and another to indicate things that maybe aren't the best way to serve. In a journal, describe why each option was either a good way to serve or not the best way.

- Take a selfie with the person you're serving and post on social media.

- Smile, give a hug, or invite into your group of friends someone who's lonely or in need.

- Complain about the surroundings as you help.

- Photograph the area you're serving and talk about the rough conditions you've experienced while there.

- Give up a day of winter break to serve at a homeless shelter, food pantry, or clothing drive.

- Say you don't have anything to give, so you just can't serve.

- Practice generosity, even if it means giving your time rather than your money.

day 18

THE RIGHTEOUS POOR

discover|

READ PROVERBS 28:6.

Better the poor person who lives with integrity than the rich one who distorts right and wrong.

If given the choice between being rich or poor, most people would choose to be rich. Wealth does provide certain comforts and opportunities. However, wealth can also distort our view of right and wrong. Sometimes those who are rich believe they are "above the law" or can buy their way out of trouble. But today's verse explains that it's better to be poor and have integrity than to be wealthy and have a corrupted view of right and wrong.

Clearly, not all rich people distort right and wrong, and some poor people have a backward morality as well. This proverb is not saying that poverty is better than wealth. Wealth, like anything, must be submitted to the Lordship of Christ. Anything that we allow to take center stage in our lives can cause us distort right and wrong. The point is that godly integrity is more important than our wealth, the brands we buy, or the friends we have.

Ultimately, wealth is infinitely less important than your integrity. When you stand before God one day, He will be totally unimpressed with the stuff you collected during your lifetime. He created the world, so in reality, He owns it all already.

delight |

How can wealth—or anything else we place before God—cause us to distort what is right and wrong?

Why do you think the poor person with integrity is better off than the wealthy person without it?

display |

We live in a temporary world awaiting eternity in God's coming kingdom. When we compromise our conscience and ignore the Holy Spirit's conviction, we may succeed temporarily, but not in ways that really matter. Doing sinful things that help us in worldly terms means we fail where it matters forever. The good news is that grace can be found in Jesus when we repent of what we've done wrong.

If you are struggling with envy toward the girls who have more than you, let it go. Give it to God right now. If you have watched people who distort right and wrong succeed in this life, let God deal with them and focus your own heart on Him. On an index card, write out: *I will focus on making sure I walk in integrity as I love and serve others. I will focus on submitting my own heart to God's will.* When you're tempted to feel jealous of what others have—and angry when they achieve their wealth or success unethically—look at these words and remind yourself that God is in control.

Today's verse says that it is better to have your integrity even if you have little. Journal two visions of your future self: one where are wealthy and one where you aren't. Pray that no matter where you end up, you will be a godly woman of integrity who shows kindness to those who have less—physically or spiritually.

Make the commitment to God in prayer that, regardless of how much or how little you have as an adult, you will always have integrity.

day 19

LITTLE + RIGHTEOUSNESS = BETTER

discover |

READ PSALM 37:1-29.

The little that the righteous person has is better than the abundance of many wicked people. — Psalm 37:16

King David, the author of Psalm 37, was a master at blending the wisdom of God with the beauty of poetry. This psalm speaks to the truth that wickedness is meaningless—the wicked will not gain anything in the long-run; in fact, they'll actually lose everything.

Four times David explained who would "inherit the land" (vv. 9,11, 22,29). Those who would inherit the land weren't the wicked; instead, they were the ones who put their hope in the Lord, the humble, those blessed by the Lord, and the righteous. In each situation, David emphasized that our posture before the Lord is what's really matters.

Our previous devotion focused on integrity being greater than material wealth. This verse focuses on the material wealth of the righteous, contrasting it with the material wealth of the wicked. What we do with what we have indicates what is happening in our hearts—for better or for worse. The righteous person will use even what little he or she has to honor God by showing kindness to others, while the wicked will use their abundant wealth for fruitless or evil endeavors. Once again, God's word plainly reveals it's better to have little and be righteous before God than to have much and be wicked.

delight |

If someone lives righteously before God, what will ultimately come from their material wealth on earth regardless of how much they have?

What good will riches be to the wicked when they come to the end of their lives and see God face to face?

display |

The righteous person in Psalm 37:16 may not have much, but she will show kindness to those in need because of the Holy Spirit who lives inside of her. Only the Holy Spirit can transform the wicked person into the righteous person—and every righteous person was once wicked.

Write out the characteristics of those David said would "inherit the land." In a journal, write out how you can cultivate godly humility, grow in righteousness, put your hope in the Lord even when life is tough, and how the Lord has blessed you recently.

Ultimately, we must see everything we have as belonging to God. Whether it is much or little, it's His. We must also believe that God is the great multiplier. He can take even a little bit and do great things with it (Matt. 14:18-21). List three ways you can use whatever resources you have (great or small) to show kindness to others.

Talk honestly to God about what you have and what you will have one day. Ask God to help you see that whatever you have or will have will always belong to God. Make it your heart's desire to use whatever you have for righteousness rather than wickedness.

Choose Kindness

JUSTICE AND THE JUDGE

discover |

READ PSALM 140:12-13.

I know that the LORD upholds the just cause of the poor, justice for the needy.
—*Psalm 140:12*

Statements about injustice assume that rights were violated or promises were broken. So, any meaningful statement about justice assumes that someone gave us rights or made us promises. The ideals that guide nations with justice systems must draw their authority from an ultimate understanding of justice in the universe. Where there is justice, there is the Judge. Ultimately, justice derives from the existence of a real God who cares about people and created our understanding of right and wrong.

Unfortunately, modern society has ignored God's place as the Judge, but still longs for justice. We all innately (naturally) have the same general sense of what is right and what is wrong. When societies turn their backs on God, they fail. We see countless examples of this throughout history. (God's own people even fell into slavery and exile when they turned away from Him.)

However, the gospel always gives us hope. God has brought revival to failing nations in the past. Christians today can reintroduce the forgotten gospel that gives true hope to the poor—not hope in a government system that cannot change hearts, but in a Savior whose Spirit permanently transforms souls.

delight |

How does God uphold the cause of the poor and give justice to the needy today?

What role should the church play in upholding the cause of the poor and seeking justice for the needy?

display |

Those in power will answer to God for what they did for the poor and needy in their care. You may not be in a position of power, but God's Spirit is in you. You can speak these words of hope to those who are victims of injustice, circumstance, or even their own sin. God cares about the poor. He hears their cries and upholds their cause. We are called to join Him in this mission.

When your friends or classmates talk about justice, direct the conversation to the ultimate origins of justice itself. Get down to the very roots of where justice comes from in the first place. God created justice and put it in our hearts to long for it. In a journal, write out a general idea of what you might say so you can be prepared when the opportunity arises.

Use pages 64-65 to help you memorize today's Scripture. When you see headlines about needy people being oppressed, let it remind you God's position on the matter. Let it lead you to take the same position. Live out your calling to uphold the cause of the poor and seek justice for the needy.

> Ask God to give you hope for ultimate justice to be done one day for those in need. Profess to Him your belief that these words are absolutely true and let them give you peace—then share that peace with others.

Choose Kindness

Simple Acts of Kindness

Kindness isn't just a topic of discussion in the Bible, and it's more than a character trait or superlative. Kindness is a choice to take action. Maybe you've heard stories of people buying someone else's coffee, gas, or food and put those ideas on a pedestal of the best ways to show kindness. While those are great things to do for others if you can, there are simple, everyday ways we can show kindness, too.

Here are Fifteen Ways to Choose Kindness Today

1 Carry groceries inside for an elderly neighbor.

2 Offer to babysit for a single mom or young couple— for free!

3 Write a thank-you note to someone who showed you kindness.

4 Invite the new kid to sit with you at lunch or at church.

5 Pay a compliment to someone you don't know.

6 Try not to complain about anything for the whole day.

7 Give your time to someone who's lonely.

8 Go through your clothes and donate anything you've outgrown or don't wear often.

9 If someone else begins to gossip, don't participate. Instead, encourage them to go directly to that person or not to talk about them.

10 Set aside your phone when spending time with your family and friends.

11 Do a shout out post for one person each day this month on social media, sharing about what makes them awesome!

12 Think about your favorite songs, podcasts, movies, books, and videos. Consider which of your friends might enjoy them and send them a link or let them borrow the book or movie.

13 Ask your pastor for the name of a senior adult who might be a shut-in or doesn't have family in the area. Begin building a relationship with this person; it'll be good for you, too!

14 Buy an extra coffee or hot chocolate and give it to someone you know is having a tough day. Consider finding out their favorite flavor and buying that. Attach a short note or encouraging Bible verse.

15 Say thank you to people who don't hear it often—like the people who clean the restrooms at your school or serve the food. Consider writing them a note too.

Now it's your turn. Ask God to show you how you can use the gifts He's given you to show kindness to others. Think about your life, the people around you, and the opportunities you have to choose kindness. Make a list of at least five more simple ways you can show kindness.

CARING COMMANDS

discover

> Thank God for His heart toward the poor and the immigrants.
> Lift up the needs of the poor and immigrants today.

READ LEVITICUS 23:22.

"When you reap the harvest of your land, you are not to reap all the way to the edge of your field or gather the gleanings of your harvest. Leave them for the poor and the resident alien; I am the LORD your God."

Israel is a unique nation—the Old Testament established it as a nation led by God Himself. This is a theocracy (pronounced "thee-'ah-crah-see"), and their laws were actually written by God. One of those laws called them to care for the poor and the immigrants by allowing them to gather what was leftover after each harvest.

This law played a key role in the coming of the Messiah. In the Book of Ruth, an immigrant widow (Ruth) from an enemy nation followed her mother-in-law to her home in Bethlehem. She arrived just in time for the barley harvest. Because the farmers observed this law, she and her mother-in-law had more than enough to eat.

But this was about far more than a meal. The owner of the field was a man named Boaz and the young widow was named Ruth. These were the great-grandparents of King David, but their greatest descendant is Jesus. Ruth and Boaz met were because of the command in today's verse and Boaz commitment to show kindness to the needy.

delight |

Why do you think God reminded His people that He is the Lord at the end of this command?

What does this command reveal about God's heart toward the poor and the immigrants in ancient Israel's day?

What does this command reveal about God's heart toward the poor and the immigrants today?

display |

No matter what nations require regarding their poor and immigrants, Christians are called to care for them. Only the gospel can transform a heart and fill a former sinner with the Holy Spirit, which leads to acts of kindness toward the marginalized. No modern law that provides assistance for an immigrant can address the spiritual needs of the downtrodden: only Jesus can do that. So, Christians of all nations have to step up.

Speak to your parent, guardian, and/or ministry leader about ways your church can help to care for immigrants. Write out a few ways you can start helping now.

Also ask about or research ministries in the area that care for the poor. Find ways you can help and get involved!

MAKER OF ALL

discover|

> Ask the Holy Spirit to reveal to you any prejudice in your heart toward those on the other end of the wealth spectrum from you and your family, whether rich or poor. Listen closely to how He convicts you, and prepare your heart to read God's Word on the matter.

READ PROVERBS 22:1-2.

Rich and poor have this in common: the LORD makes them all. –Proverbs 22:2

Our spiritual need for a Savior is an incredible equalizer. All the wealth in the world couldn't save a sinner and even the most virtuous poor person in the world still needs Jesus. Whether we spend our lives accumulating impressive things or we spend our lives giving away all that we have, we are all born equally sinful and in need of a Savior.

Note the stark contrast at the beginning of this verse and the unifying truth at the end. We all need this reminder from time to time. Those who look down on the poor need to know that their wealth does not give them greater standing in the eyes of God. Those who have struggled materially in this world should recognize the wealthy as their fellow creations. While many want to label people as many ways as possible, today's Scripture reminds us of two simple truths—God made everyone and the ground is level at the foot of the cross. What beautiful truths to keep in mind!

delight |

Why do you think our culture assigns different values to people based on how wealthy they are?

How might a right understanding of this verse influence the practice of valuing people based on their income?

What else do the rich and poor have in common?

display |

Let this verse shape your view wealth inequality: All wealth and all poverty are temporary, but salvation is eternal. People have value because they are made in the image of God and loved by Him—not because of the amount of stuff they have. Seek to not view the wealthy with jealousy, hatred, or undue admiration. Seek to not view the poor with disdain or as saints. Commit to viewing all people as creations of our loving God in need of salvation.

Because both the wealthy and the poor came from the same Creator, they will also answer to the same Judge. Hopefully, they will know and be answering to the Judge as their Savior. List three steps you can take to give money the appropriate level of focus and importance in your heart.

Keep mental track of the ways you speak to people based on their wealth. If you find yourself speaking more kindly to wealthy people and less charitably toward poor people, confess that before God and repent. Then, think about how you can respond differently in the future.

day 23

FAVORITISM

discover

Ask for God's forgiveness for any times you've shown favoritism in the past. Allow today's Scripture to guide your thoughts toward God's feelings about favoritism.

READ JAMES 2:1-13.

Listen, my dear brothers and sisters: Didn't God choose the poor in this world to be rich in faith and heirs of the kingdom that he has promised to those who love him? — James 2:5

God's Word calls us out if we treat poor people differently from the way we treat rich people. James calls it showing favoritism. Verse 5 is directed at people whose economic system worked differently from ours. Today, it is possible to earn money and not oppress anyone in the process. The wealthy original recipients of James obtained their wealth through oppressing others, and he called them out for it!

Under the inspiration of the Holy Spirit, James went on to write, "...you show favoritism, you commit sin and are convicted by the law as transgressors" (v. 9). This teaching reminds the rich of the infinite value the poor have in God's eyes. The poor have a dependency on God that is difficult for the rich to grasp. James also challenged the rich to see the poor through God's eyes. Anyone who loves God is an heir to His kingdom and worthy of love, regardless of her economic status.

delight |

How is it possible for people to be poor financially but rich in faith?

Heirs are people who inherit wealth from their parents. What does it mean that the poor can be "heirs of the kingdom"?

A promise is only as good as the integrity of the promise-maker. Why can we trust the promise found in James 2:5?

display |

Think about ways you might unintentionally show favoritism in your school, student ministry, family, and social circles. List three ideas to help you stop showing favoritism and begin showing kindness to all people.

If you been guilty of looking down on those who happen to have come from families with fewer material blessings than yours, ask God to help you see the poor who love God as heirs to a kingdom greater than the greatest wealth in the world. Write out your commitment to treating them like the heirs they are.

day 24

A DIFFERENT WAY

discover |

READ LUKE 6:20-26.

Then looking up at his disciples, he said: Blessed are you who are poor, because the kingdom of God is yours. Blessed are you who are hungry now, because you will be filled. Blessed are you who weep now, because you will laugh.
— *Luke 6:20-21*

Have you ever asked your parents for help with homework and heard them say, "This isn't how I learned _____!" To help you, they have to learn a completely different way to do things. In many ways, this is how people felt when Jesus came on the scene. His teaching was different from what was accepted as normal. This is the setting for the Scripture for today.

As He did in Matthew 5-7, in Luke 6 Jesus turned the common cultural thinking completely upside down and showed all of us just how drastically we fall short of the biblical Law. This reveals our profound need for a Savior! But His words gave hope to an oppressed people by turning their weary eyes heavenward to the kingdom awaiting those who place their faith in Him. That same hope remains today. There is no affliction brought on by hunger, poverty, or sadness that is not completely eclipsed by the incredible glory of heaven (2 Cor. 4:17).

delight |

How could knowing that there is no hunger in heaven bring comfort today?

What are some other examples of Jesus' teaching that are opposite to what is accepted as normal to society? (*Hint: Keep reading Luke 6.*)

display |

In Luke 6:20, Jesus told the believing poor that the kingdom of heaven was theirs! As you take action to show kindness to the marginalized, don't forget to meet their eternal need for knowing Jesus even as you help fulfill their temporary needs.

With your parent or guardian's permission and supervision, purchase a $10 gift card from a fast food restaurant and give it to someone asking for help on the street. Explain that you are giving them this gift because you love them and because Jesus loves them too. Listen to their story and don't judge why they are in the situation they are in. See if you can continue a relationship with them and seek to meet both their physical and spiritual needs.

If you are hungry, weeping, or poor right now—hold onto Jesus' words. Let Him speak directly to your broken heart through today's passage. Read Revelation 21:1-7 to get a glimpse of what awaits you in heaven, and let the brilliant light bursting from that glimpse obliterate the darkness you may feel. God will provide for your needs. He always has. He always will.

Think about a girl you know who may be hurting deeply. Write a note of encouragement to her, and include this verse. Consider sending the note with a gift card for coffee, a plate of cookies, or the gift of your time.

Ask God for opportunities to show kindness to those in need—kindness that includes the gospel. Profess your belief to Him that what He said is true.

IGNORING ISN'T BLISS

discover |

> Thank God for providing you and your family what you
> need to get through the day. Ask Him to prepare your
> heart to help feed the homeless in your city.

READ PROVERBS 28:27.

*The one who gives to the poor will not be in need, but one who turns his eyes
away will receive many curses.*

It is so easy to turn and look away from problems we could solve
and people we could help. Sometimes, helping is tough. But God
did not turn and look the other way from us—He gave His only Son
as a sacrifice for our sins. This reality obligates us to show kindness
and love.

This is an Old Testament text, meaning it was taught under the
old covenant before Jesus. But what it teaches us about the heart,
character, and nature of God still applies. The ancient wisdom of
Proverbs will never be irrelevant.

The first half of the verse reveals something powerful about
God's provision for those who are kind and generous to the
poor. The curses in the second half of the verse are described
as "many" because someone who turned his eyes away from
the poor and refused to help was in complete disobedience
to the Old Testament Law. While we are no longer under the
Old Testament Law, God's righteous anger with those who see the
poor and then look away, remains.

delight |

Why will the one who gives to the poor not be in need?

What does the act of turning our eyes away indicate about our hearts?

This verse reveals the necessity of generosity and selflessness for followers of Christ. How can you cultivate generosity and selflessness in your life?

display |

Choose not to look away, even though looking away would be easier. Thank God for the ways in which you are not in need. Thank Him for the blessings He gave you after you blessed others—even blessings you did not realize He had given you until you read today's Scripture.

Working with your parent or guardian and ministry leader, volunteer to feed the homeless through a licensed and established facility. When you do, make it a point to look people in the eye and take any opportunity that may come to hear their stories. Brace yourself: their stories will not likely be G-rated. Keep in mind not to judge them for where they are, just love them and seek to make a friend. Jesus meets us where we are, and we should seek to meet others where they are too!

Confess to God any times you've been tempted to look away when you knew you could help. Look back at pages 52-53. Choose one of the 15 ways to choose kindness and act on it today.

I KNOW THAT
THE LORD
UPHOLDS
THE JUST
CAUSE OF THE
POOR,
JUSTICE FOR
THE NEEDY.

PSALM 140:12

day 26

discover

READ DEUTERONOMY 15:1-11..

> *"Give to him, and don't have a stingy heart when you give, and because of this the LORD your God will bless you in all your work and in everything you do. For there will never cease to be poor people in the land; that is why I am commanding you, 'Open your hand willingly to your poor and needy brother in your land.'"* — Deuteronomy 15:10-11

Have you ever read two verses from the Bible that seem to directly contradict one another? Deuteronomy 15:4-5 gave Israel instructions for how they could eliminate poverty completely. These instructions were dependent upon their complete and careful obedience to everything God commanded. If they obeyed God's command they could accomplish the goal of having no poor (v. 4). Then, seven verses later, Scripture says there will always be poor people.

That might seem a little confusing, but here's the thing: God knows us. Because God knew they were (and we are) incapable of obeying everything He commanded, they would (and will) always have poor people. Still, the economic instructions in this passage to teach us how to eliminate poverty. Notice how this path is not a cold set of bland instructions. No, God's instructions were to care for the poor and to give from their hearts—hearts that were not stingy and selfish. It's so important to realize that our hearts must be compassionate and generous if we want to truly care for the poor.

delight |

Why does the heart of the giver matter to God? Why is it not enough to just give?

God's instructions for Israel's hearts became their nation's laws. How should people who live in nations without such laws take care of their poor?

> Ask God for an opportunity to earn some money that you will then use to give to the poor.

display |

When you receive a paycheck, if you have not already, you may see a portion taken out before it comes to you. Some of that deduction goes toward taxes that give assistance to help the poor. But, we can't sit back and think we've fulfilled God's command to care for the poor because of this. Christians are called to give to our churches and our churches are called to use some of these resources to serve the poor in your community. Ask your church staff about ways your church helps the poor in your community. Then, do what you can to get involved.

If you don't have a job, find ways to give your time to serve the poor. Whether that's volunteering at a homeless shelter, organizing a closet for ministries that receive donations, or offering free babysitting for a single parent in your church. Come up with a list of ways you might be able to serve the poor. Make sure to go over this list with a parent or guardian before you set out to serve.

START OFF RIGHT

discover|

READ PROVERBS 31:8-9.

Speak up for those who have no voice, for the justice of all who are dispossessed.
—Proverbs 31:8

If you've ever danced, sung or played a solo, then you know how important it is to start off in the right key. If even one instrument plays in the wrong key, they entire song gets thrown off. Even the most seasoned musicians start in the wrong key sometimes, but they stop, and start over. Still, the goal is to know the right key and start of playing it. Like sheet music tells us what key a song should be in, today's Scripture was intended to help a young king begin his reign the right way.

Except for young royals who inherited their thrones at an early age, every person who has ever been in power has had to wait for it. While you might not yet be in charge of anything or old enough to make important decisions, that does not mean you are powerless. You can start off on the right foot now. If you don't speak up at this stage in your life for those who have no voice—people like the unborn, the poor, and the truly marginalized—you will not suddenly start speaking for them when you are an adult and potentially in a position of influence. Make it your habit today to speak up and speak truth on behalf of those who remain unheard.

delight |

Verse 9 calls for us to "defend the cause of the oppressed and needy." Who are the oppressed and needy in our culture?

Using whatever influence you might have, what steps can you take today to speak up for those who have no voice?

display |

Find your voice and speak up boldly about the freedom you've found in Jesus. So much of what we talk about is meaningless in eternity (Ecc. 6:11), and we need to talk about what matters, too. Our words, like our actions, should reflect our Creator. Here are a few tips to speak boldly from the freedom you have in Jesus.

- Make sure you understand what others are truly saying, not just what you think they said.

- Refuse to gossip or spread rumors and stop others when they try to speak poorly of others.

- Be courageous—don't be afraid to sign your name to what you believe in.

- Know that persecution may come when you speak up for biblical truth—even from other Christians who are afraid to speak up themselves.

Highlight the item from the list that you think might be most difficult for you. Journal your thoughts and feelings. Make it a prayer to God, asking Him to fill you with a holy strength and courage to start off right—learning to speak His truth today—no matter what!

Invite others to join you in speaking up. Encourage them not for your own glory or recognition, but for God's!

Ask God to break your heart for the things that break His heart. Pray that you would have the boldness to speak up for justice when the time comes and that you will speak in love.

day 28

PRAYERS OF POOR

discover |

READ PSALM 102:12-17.

He will pay attention to the prayer of the destitute and will not despise their prayer. — Psalm 102:17

Have you ever taken a device apart because it was broken, fixed it, and then put it back together again? It is amazing to see the inner-workings of something that was designed for a specific purpose. You can clean out the dust and lint that does not belong. You can meticulously repair it and watch it come back to its original purpose. This is what God was doing with Israel when today's text was written.

The psalmist who wrote this was in despair and crying out to God, even while continuing to believe and trust in these beautiful truths about God. The verse immediately before this verse gives important context, "for the LORD will rebuild Zion; he will appear in his glory." The name "Zion" refers to Israel and, just like the text prophesied, God did indeed rebuild her.

> If you have felt or currently feel "destitute" (poor or down), let the truth of this verse wash over you. Believe it. God knows all about your troubles and this verse clearly shows that He is listening. He loves you. So, talk to Him.

delight |

To despise means to view something as worthless or ignore it. Since God does not despise the prayers of the destitute, He would view them as valuable and worth His time and attention. How does it affect you to know that God values your prayers?

In Psalm 102:1-2, the psalmist speaks very plainly and directly to God. What is the difference between speaking honestly with God and speaking disrespectfully to Him?

display |

As difficult as it is to understand, sometimes God allows us to walk through difficult days. Eventually, the things we learned during those tough days will help us—or someone else—through a time of struggle. Whether we are in good days or "destitute" days, we must believe that God is still good and with us even when we find ourselves like the psalmist and crying out in anguish. List a few ways you can remind yourself that God is good even on the tough days.

Listen to the song "Goodness of God" by Jenn Johnson. Make this your prayer to God, praising Him for His never-ending, never-failing goodness in your life.

Showing kindness to the destitute around you might include sharing this passage of Scripture with them, praying with them, or simply sitting and listening to them. Look for someone around you who is struggling. Ask God how you can be an encouragement to them. Then, obey and reach out. God wants us to bear one another's burdens.

day 29

TOUGH TRUTHS

discover |

> Thank Jesus for giving Himself up for you. Commit to
> giving to Him what can.

READ 2 CORINTHIANS 8:7-15.

*For you know the grace of our Lord Jesus Christ: Though he was rich, for your
sake he became poor, so that by his poverty you might become rich.*
— 2 Corinthians 8:9

Many critics of Christianity often say that all pastors ever talk
about at church is money. While it's not all that is ever discussed at
church, it's an important element. Pastors know the needs of the
church, community, and even the world. These needs are met by
the tithes and offerings of the people of the church. Our churches
can't meet these needs if we aren't giving.

In the Scripture for today, Paul reminded the church at Corinth
that Jesus gave everything for us! Earlier, the Corinthian church
had pledged to give an offering for the needs of the Macedonian
church. So, Paul asked to them to complete the gift and give
generously the way Jesus gave generously. When we grasp what
Jesus did for us—sacrificing Himself completely—we are more
likely to surrender everything to Him, including our finances.

delight |

This verse isn't a promise that God will give you lots of money. What did Paul mean by "rich?"

Why did Paul describe Jesus' descent from the wealth of heaven to the poverty of earth as "grace?"

Describe what happens in your heart when you read the words "for your sake."

display |

Read 2 Corinthians 9:12. Giving is a form of both kindness and worship. Pray for your pastor the next time he has to encourage the church to give. Sympathize with the responsibility of the God-driven position he is in as he pursues the same mission as Paul was when he wrote to the Corinthians 2,000 years ago. Write a quick note of encouragement to your pastor, thanking him for speaking truth even when it's tough or unpopular.

Each time you earn money, start giving at least 10 percent of it to your church's general budget. Do it with the same cheerful heart Paul describes in these chapters of 2 Corinthians. Think about the ways God will use it to advance His kingdom and know there is no better use of our money. It is all God's anyway—just like our hearts.

If you don't have a job right now, look for ways you can give your time to your church—maybe volunteering to work in the nursery or kids ministry, running slides for the worship team, or welcoming visitors as they walk through the doors.

day 30

PROPHECY AND DISBELIEF

discover|

READ LUKE 4:16-21.

The scroll of the prophet Isaiah was given to him, and unrolling the scroll, he found the place where it was written: The Spirit of the Lord is on me, because he has anointed me to preach good news to the poor. He has sent me to proclaim release to the captives and recovery of sight to the blind, to set free the oppressed, to proclaim the year of the Lord's favor. — Luke 4:17-19

Have you ever seen old social media posts by celebrities from before they were famous, in which they claimed that they would one day become exactly what they are today? It is incredibly inspiring. It is also satisfying, and yet sad, to read the hateful comments on those posts from the now embarrassed people who told them that they were crazy. On an eternally greater scale, the same thing happened with Jesus.

After Jesus said this to the people at the synagogue in his old hometown of Nazareth, He sat down (which was the traditional posture of teaching) and said, "Today as you listen, this Scripture has been fulfilled" (v. 21). While they were impressed with His gracious words (v. 22), they did not believe Him and eventually tried to push Him off a cliff for what He said (v. 30)! Jesus did every single thing this ancient prophecy said the Messiah would do, including preach good news to the poor.

For a man coming to change the world, beginning His public life with a declaration of ministry to the poor doesn't seem like the greatest strategy. But Jesus was anything but ordinary in everything He did.

---

delight |

What type of captivity do you think Jesus came to release people from?

Why do you think Jesus focused His ministry on the poor and the outcast?

> Just take a moment and focus your heart on Jesus, your Savior. Praise Him for His kindness to you and ask Him to help you be kind to others in return.

display |

Read Galatians 5:22-23. List out the fruit of the Spirit. Highlight kindness as a reminder to keep choosing kindness even though you've finished this devotional.

List two major ways God has softened your heart to choose kindness over these 30 days.

List five things you can do to continue to live in kindness.

Even If...

We were created with the ability to reason and choose. Think about the way sin entered the world, it was through the choice Adam and Eve made to disobey God (Gen. 3:6). Yes, Satan tempted them, but ultimately, they knew what God had said and they chose to ignore it in favor of what they wanted in that moment (Gen. 2:17). When we're faced with the temptation to respond in kindness or some other (likely sinful) way, we can choose to be kind.

One critical note here before we dig into some responses Scripture demonstrates for us: You can be hurt and be kind, and you can also disagree and be kind.

Now, let's take a look at some different scenarios Scripture gives for choosing kindness.

I can choose kindness when someone mistreats me.
"Bless those who curse you, pray for those who mistreat you."
—Luke 6:28

I can choose kindness when I face persecution for my faith.
Bless those who persecute you; bless and do not curse.
—Romans 12:14

I can choose kindness when someone gossips about me.
Keep your tongue from evil and your lips from deceitful speech.
—Psalm 34:13

Remind them to submit to rulers and authorities, to obey, to be ready for every good work, to slander no one, to avoid fighting, and to be kind, always showing gentleness to all people.
 —Titus 3:1-2

I can choose kindness by not gossiping about someone else.
Without wood, fire goes out; without a gossip, conflict dies down.
—Proverbs 26:20

I can choose kindness by speaking the truth about others to defeat rumors and lies.
"You must not spread a false report. Do not join the wicked to be a malicious witness."
— Exodus 23:1

I can choose kindness by standing up for those who are bullied, mistreated, left out, or overlooked.
Speak up for those who have no voice, for the justice of all who are dispossessed. Speak up, judge righteously, and defend the cause of the oppressed and needy.
—Proverbs 31:8-9

Learn to do what is good. Pursue justice. Correct the oppressor. Defend the rights of the fatherless. Plead the widow's cause.
—Isaiah 1:17

I can choose kindness by avoiding crude jokes.
Obscene and foolish talking or crude joking are not suitable, but rather giving thanks.
—Ephesians 5:4

Avoid irreverent and empty speech, since those who engage in it will produce even more godlessness, and their teaching will spread like gangrene.
—2 Timothy 2:16-17a

I can choose kindness by not arguing with others over things that don't matter.
But reject foolish and ignorant disputes, because you know that they breed quarrels. The Lord's servant must not quarrel, but must be gentle to everyone, able to teach, and patient, instructing his opponents with gentleness.
—2 Timothy 2:23-25

I can choose kindness by speaking compassionately to others.
Pleasant words are a honeycomb: sweet to the taste and health to the body.
—Proverbs 16:24

I can choose kindness by being a good friend.
A friend loves at all times, and a brother is born for a difficult time.
—Proverbs 17:17

I can choose kindness by speaking the truth in love.
But speaking the truth in love, let us grow in every way into him who is the head—Christ.
—Ephesians 4:15

I can choose kindness by choosing to love others like Jesus would.
Love is patient, love is kind.
—1 Corinthians 13:4a

I can choose kindness by forgiving others—no matter what they've done.
And be kind and compassionate to one another, forgiving one another, just as God also forgave you in Christ.
—Ephesians 4:32

Therefore, as God's chosen ones, holy and dearly loved, put on compassion, kindness, humility, gentleness, and patience, bearing with one another and forgiving one another if anyone has a grievance against another. Just as the Lord has forgiven you, so you are also to forgive.
—Colossians 3:12-13

Your Turn

What are some other scenarios where you might need to choose kindness?
Support your answer(s) with Scripture.

Choose Kindness

Sources

1. Max Anders (2012). HNTC Vol. 08: Galatians, Ephesians, Philippians & Colossians. B&H Publishing Group. Retrieved from https://app.wordsearchbible.lifeway.com.
2. Random Acts of Kindness, "Kindness Health Facts," February 11, 2016, https://www.dartmouth.edu/wellness/emotional/rakhealthfacts.pdf.